The publishers of this volume dedicate it to lovers of classical music the world over. This includes outstanding contributions to classical music lore in easy piano format, to be enjoyed by pianists both young and mature.

The compositions in this book have been carefully selected as notable works by some of the greatest composers of the classical tradition. Spanning over 250 years, from Bach to Rachmaninoff, players can enjoy an inspiring journey through the history of classical music and gain further insight from the selected composer biographies.

All the pieces in this book have been arranged in easy piano format in a considered and thoughtful fashion, retaining as much of the original musical substance as possible. Marks of phrasing and expression are often editorial additions, especially in earlier music. These signs were added for a quicker, easier understanding of the structure and mood of the compositions thus should be considered as suggestions rather than precise directions. The student should always defer to the judgement of their teacher.

It is our sincere hope that you will enjoy playing the delightful piano miniatures contained within this volume, whether it be for study, recital, sight reading, or just relaxing musical entertainment of the highest calibre.

The Publisher

PIANO PIECES
ALPHABETICAL CONTENTS

PIANO PIECES
CONTENTS BY COMPOSER

Compiled by James Welland and Andrew Skirrow.
Edited by Sam Lung and James Welland.
Music engraved and processed by Camden Music Services.
Additional introductory texts by James Welland.
Designed by Raissa Pardini.
Front cover illustration re-drawn by Sergio Sandoval.

Order Number AM1011571
Printed in the EU.

ISBN: 978-1-78558-252-3

Visit Hal Leonard Online at
www.halleonard.com

Contact us:
Hal Leonard
7777 West Bluemound Road
Milwaukee, WI 53213
Email: info@halleonard.com

In Europe, contact:
Hal Leonard Europe Limited
42 Wigmore Street
Marylebone, London, W1U 2RY
Email: info@halleonardeurope.com

In Australia, contact:
Hal Leonard Australia Pty. Ltd.
4 Lentara Court
Cheltenham, Victoria, 3192 Australia
Email: info@halleonard.com.au

Pastorale

Carl Philipp Emanuel Bach
1714–1788

Andantino cantabile

JOHANN SEBASTIAN
BACH

(1685–1750)

Born in Eisenach, Germany in 1685, Johann Sebastian Bach has come to be regarded as one of the great geniuses of Western music, although during his lifetime many of his contemporaries achieved greater fame. His life was spent in a succession of posts as organist and director of music in court and church establishments.

In 1708, Bach took up the post of court organist at Weimar. During his time there he composed most of his incredible number of organ works, including the famous *Toccata and Fugue in D minor*.

Successfully applying to the court of Prince Leopold of Köthen in 1717, most of Bach's compositional output was for entertainment, writing large numbers of pieces for orchestra and keyboard (harpsichord and clavichord). The six *Brandenburg Concertos* and the wonderful *Concerto for Two Violins in D minor* were written during this period. Also during this time Bach wrote the great work *The Well-Tempered Clavier*, a lengthy collection of 24 preludes and fugues written to celebrate the new well-tempered tuning system, where all the intervals on the keyboard are adjusted so that pieces in any major or minor key will sound in tune. Together with the second book, this collection is known as the '48' and is widely regarded as one of the most important bodies of work of all time for the keyboard.

In 1721, Bach married his second wife, Anna Magdalena, having 13 children in addition to the six he had had with his first wife, Maria Barbara, who had died in 1720.

Working as Kantor in St Thomas' Church in Leipzig from 1723 onward, Bach composed around 300 cantatas in all — he was required to compose a new cantata every week as part of his job. These include the famous *Jesu, Joy of Man's Desiring* and *Wachet Auf (Sleepers, Wake!)*.

In his later years Bach seemed to be setting down his lifetime's accumulation of compositional skill, demonstrating utter mastery of his art in the great epics *The Musical Offering* and *The Art of Fugue*, an exquisite example of consummate fugal writing.

By the time he died in 1750, Bach was regarded by some as old-fashioned and was criticized for his complexity. Consistently inventive, thoroughly intellectual and profoundly artistic, Bach is now regarded as one of the supreme masters of musical composition across the ages.

Toccata and Fugue in D minor

Johann Sebastian Bach
1685–1750

Minuet in G minor

Johann Sebastian Bach
1685–1750

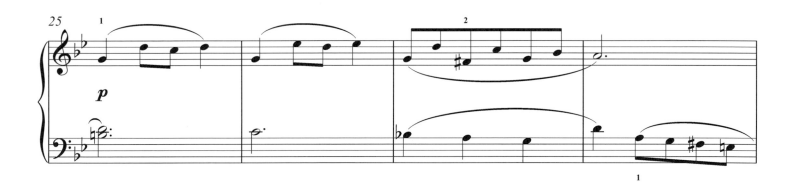

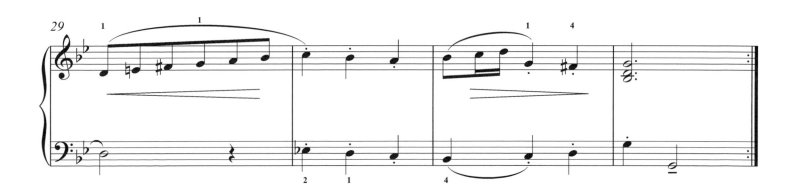

Sheep May Safely Graze

from Cantata 208

Johann Sebastian Bach
1685–1750

Andante moderato

LUDWIG VAN
BEETHOVEN

(1770–1827)

Not much is known about Beethoven's early childhood. He is said to have been a very grave and solemn boy, not mingling much with other children. He began to study the violin and piano at the age of four under the stern teaching of his father.

His general education, until he was 13, was received in a public school. After that, he was placed in the hands of the tutor Zambona. His musical education at nine years was entrusted to Pfieffer, an opera tenor, and Van den Eeden, an organist. In 1781, he studied organ with Christian Gottlob Neefe, organist in the court chapel.

Beethoven made his first journey to Vienna in 1787, where he met Mozart. Soon after, he returned to Bonn, to find his mother dying. A few months after his mother's death, his young sister died. These were dark days for Ludwig. He soon made the acquaintance of not only the Von Breuning family, who exerted a fine intellectual influence upon him, but also Count Waldstein, an important factor in his development.

In 1792, Beethoven left Bonn permanently for Vienna, where he studied for two years with Haydn, then with Schenk and finally with Albrechtsberger, who saw nothing in him at all. Here in Vienna, he was made much of by royalty and aristocracy and they gave him their constant support. He earned a comfortable living by playing, composing and by teaching, which he disliked. He also applied himself diligently to composition and concert performance.

By 1801 Beethoven was becoming prosperous, as is evidenced by an excerpt from a letter to a friend: "My compositions bring me in a great deal and I can say that I have more orders than I can execute. I have six or seven publishers for each one of my works and could have more if I chose. No more bargaining! I name my terms and they pay."

Around 1801 Beethoven began to experienced deafness, but he did not allow this to interfere with his composing. He wrote to a friend concerning this: "I will as far as possible defy my fate, though there must be moments when I shall be the most miserable of God's creatures." He was passionately fond of nature and often composed while walking in the fields.

Although a fine performer, he stands highest as a composer. He wrote nine symphonies, many quartets, sonatas, masses, concertos, one opera and many small pieces including songs.

On a return trip to Vienna in November 1825, Beethoven contracted a serious cold, which developed into inflammation of the lungs and other complications from which he continually suffered until his death, a year and a half later.

Symphony No. 5

1st movement

Ludwig van Beethoven
1770–1827

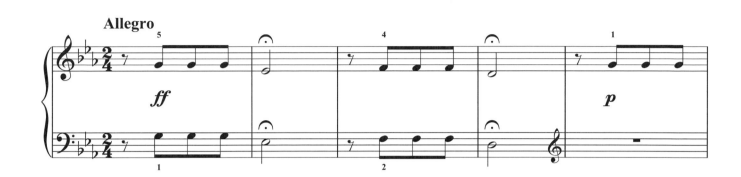

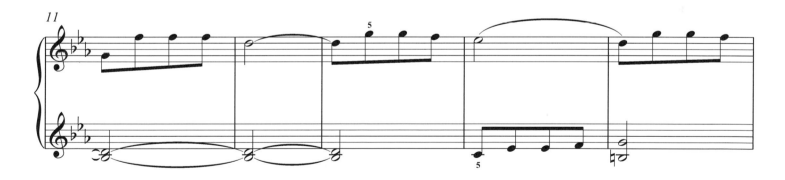

Für Elise

Ludwig van Beethoven
1770–1827

Moderately ♩ = *c.*108

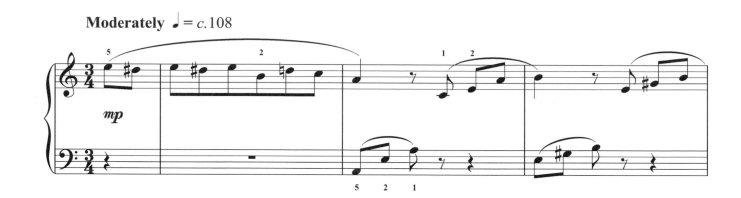

Moonlight Sonata

1st movement

Ludwig van Beethoven
1770–1827

Adagio sostenuto

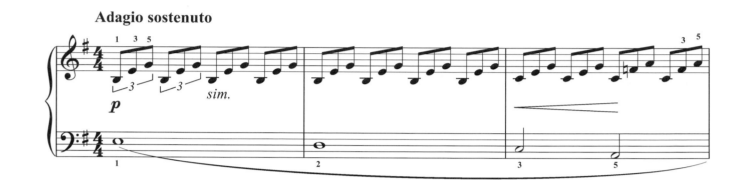

poco rit.   **a tempo**

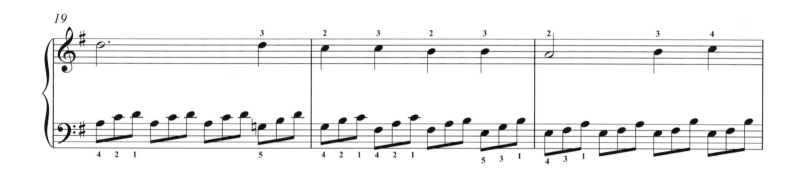

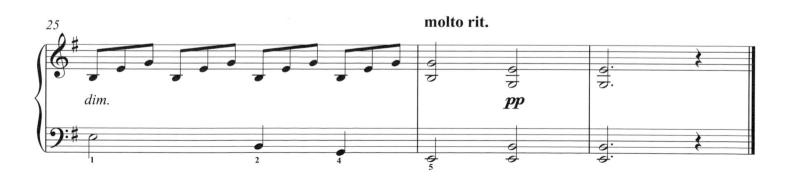

Fidelio

Ludwig van Beethoven
1770–1827

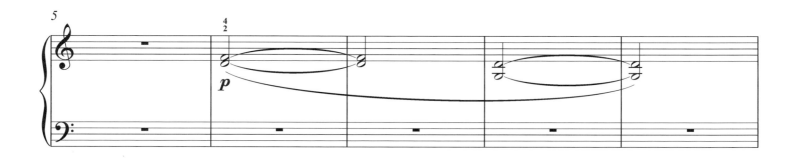

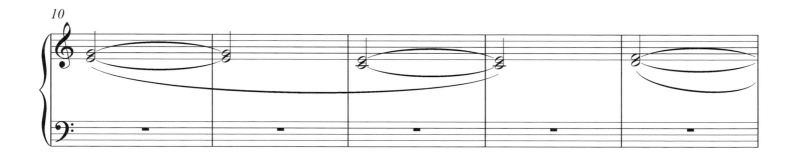

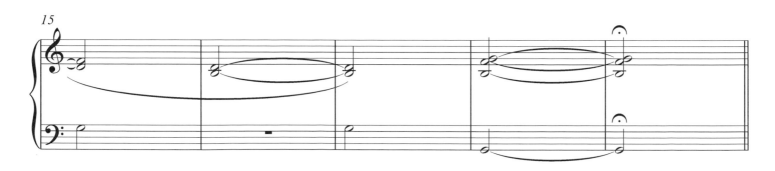

Pathétique Sonata
2nd movement

Ludwig van Beethoven
1770–1827

Prelude in E minor

Op. 2, No. 4

Georges Bizet
1838–1875

The Flower Song

from Carmen

Georges Bizet
1838–1875

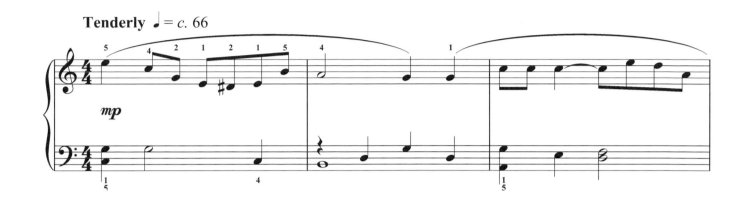

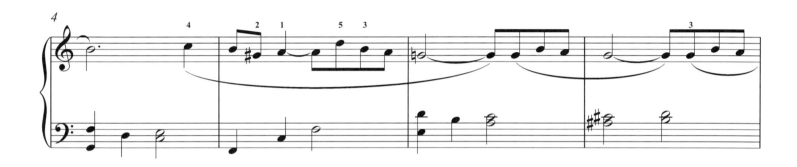

JOHANNES
BRAHMS

(1833–1897)

Johannes Brahms was the son of an excellent professional musician. His father gave him his first music lessons on the piano. At the age of 10, Brahms had already made his debut; a concert tour of America was planned for him, but he refused to go through with it. When he was 20, he went on a concert tour with Remenyi, the great Hungarian violinist, and his fame as a pianist spread far and wide.

Brahms' life was a relatively calm and quiet one, with few brainstorms or great emotional passions. An early riser, he would walk through the fields during the early morning and jot down musical ideas as they presented themselves. Then, upon his return home, he would have his coffee and then get to work, developing his ideas in composition, or teaching the piano, or practising.

He cared little for fame, and objected strongly to compliment and adulation. He had a marvellous memory, having memorised Bach and Beethoven completely, together with concert pieces by Liszt, Mendelssohn and others. His compositions were dignified, noble and in sombre colors, although his nature was ever optimistic. He was a very exacting though encouraging teacher.

Among his friends was pianist Clara Schumann, wife of Robert Schumann. He also maintained friendships with Liszt, the violinist Joachim, Antonín Dvořák, Johann Strauss and many others.

Brahms wrote in a multitude of forms: symphonies, sonatas, concertos, songs, Hungarian dances, waltzes and many others.

Waltz

Op. 39, No. 15

Johannes Brahms
1833–1897

Symphony No. 3

2nd movement

Johannes Brahms
1833–1897

Hungarian Dance No. 5

Johannes Brahms
1833–1897

FRÉDÉRIC
CHOPIN

(1810–1849)

Chopin's father was French and his mother was Polish. His father taught French at a private school attended by the children of the best families in the country, therefore Frédéric was born into a family of culture and refinement.

At a very tender age, he studied piano with Zywny. By the age of twelve he outgrew his teacher and from then on all his development in piano playing was without the aid of a teacher. When he was 14, after having composed for about six years, he started studying composition with Joseph Elsner. Meanwhile, he attended the Warsaw Lyceum and proved very brilliant in his studies, especially in Polish history and literature. He was a very lively young man and had a brilliant sense of humor.

After graduating from the Lyceum in 1827, he devoted his life to music. In 1829, he gave his first concert in Vienna, which proved successful. In 1831, he reached Paris, which was to become his permanent home. Here he met the famous literary, artistic and musical geniuses of the time as well as princes, ambassadors and the like.

In the following years in Paris, Chopin played in public very frequently and also played at recitals in the homes of aristocracy. He met Liszt, Berlioz, Hiller and many of the lesser lights. In about 1836, he met novelist Aurora Dupin, who wrote under the pen name of George Sand.

She was a very masculine type and Chopin eventually fell devotedly in love with her. They lived together with her two children until about 1837. George Sand is said to have been Chopin's inspiration, although it is known that she was unreasonable and dictatorial.

Chopin's life was marked by suffering from tuberculosis. His continual ill health caused him, in his later years, to be peevish and irritable. Notwithstanding this fact, he wrote a great many compositions for piano, said to be the best piano literature ever written.

He died, after suffering intensely for ten months, in Paris.

Grande valse brillante

Op. 18

Frédéric Chopin
1810–1849

Nocturne in E♭ major

Op. 9, No. 2

Frédéric Chopin
1810–1849

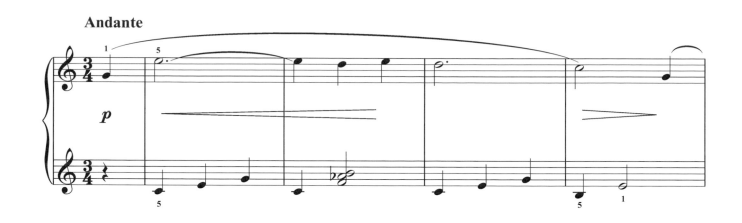

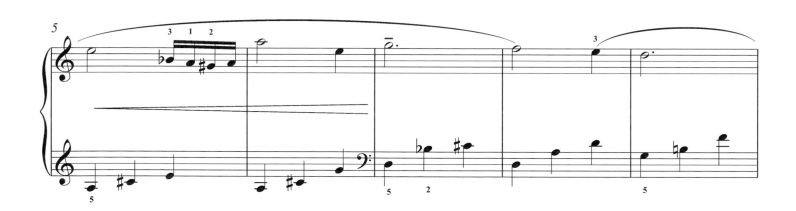

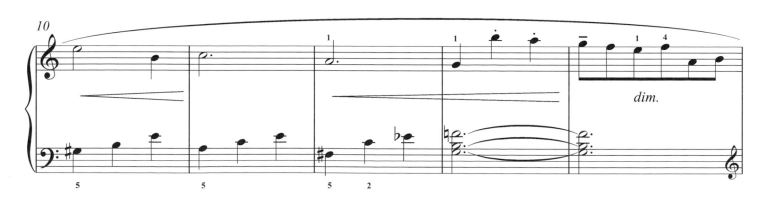

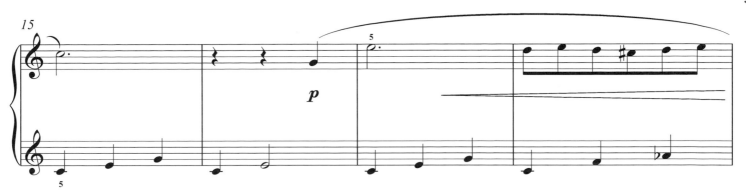

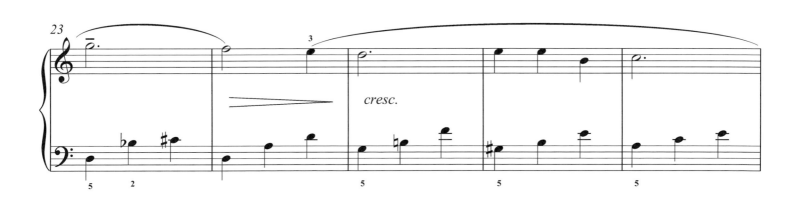

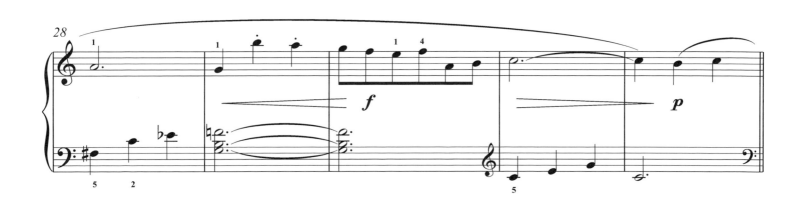

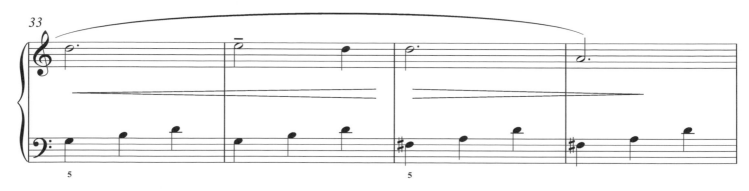

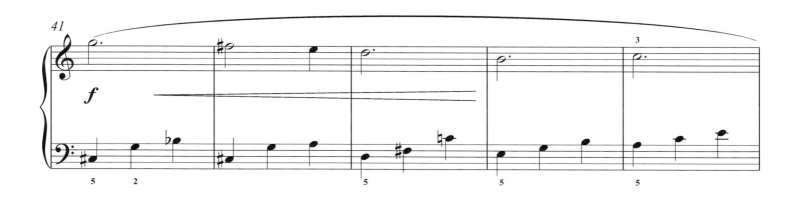

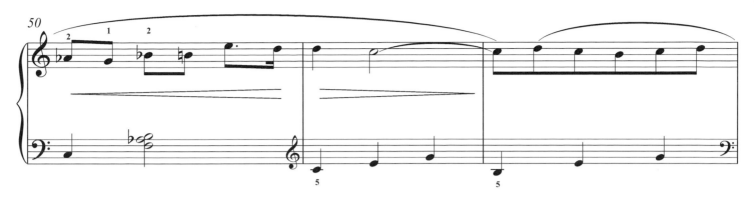

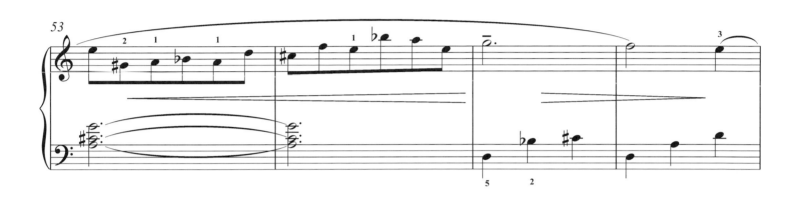

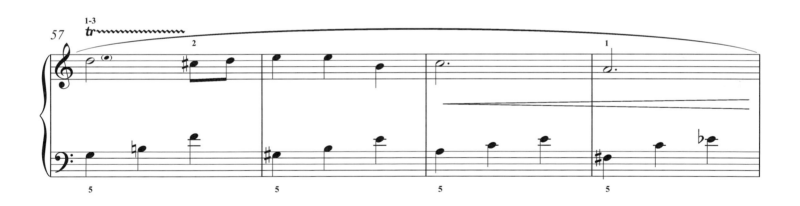

Raindrop Prelude

Op. 28, No. 15

Frédéric Chopin
1810–1849

CLAUDE
DEBUSSY

(1862–1918)

Born in 1862 in Saint-Germain-en-Laye in France, Claude-Achille Debussy was the eldest of three brothers and a sister. His parents ran a china shop before eventually moving to Paris. Times were hard and Debussy was left to his own education and could not attend school. Following his brother Eugene's death, seven-year-old Claude moved to Cannes with his sister. Aged eight he was described as being introspective, a boy who spent whole days sitting in a chair and thinking.

In Cannes, he received piano lessons, and Mme Mauté de Fleurville (a former pupil of Chopin) pronounced that he should become a musician. He entered the Paris Conservatoire aged 10, adoring the music of Berlioz, Mussorgsky and Lalo, though abhorring Beethoven. Winning the renowned Prix de Rome in 1884, he then spent three years composing for the Villa Medici, meeting other artists such as Liszt, Verdi and Boito, though returning a year early having found this a miserable experience.

In 1894, he composed the revolutionary tone-poem *Prélude à l'après-midi d'un faune*, based on Mellarmé's poem of the same name, which, along with his *String Quartet*, caused much public discussion. At the age of 40, his opera *Pelléas et Mélisande* offered confirmation that this was a composer changing musical history, with the unique lyricism of his vocal writing and lack of separate movements. Turning away from the rigidity of the Classical era's forms, Debussy was drawn to a more refined offering of emotion than was present in the Romantic era before him.

Over his musical career, Debussy made an astonishing contribution to the piano repertoire including his *Études*, his famous *Préludes* (24 pieces for solo piano, divided into two books of 12 preludes each) and other smaller pieces such as *Rêverie* and his collection of pieces written for his illegitimate daughter, Claude-Emma, *Children's Corner*.

Having said he would write his memoirs in his 60s, Debussy tragically developed cancer in 1910 and died when he was 55, in 1918. He left behind him an incredible legacy of piano, ballet, opera and orchestral music, a composer who truly exemplified the impressionist movement (though Debussy himself did not like this term) and contributed an utterly unique, influential and enduring compositional output to classical music history.

Clair de Lune

from Suite Bergamasque

Claude Debussy
1862–1918

46

En Bateau

from Petite Suite

Claude Debussy
1862–1918

Andantino

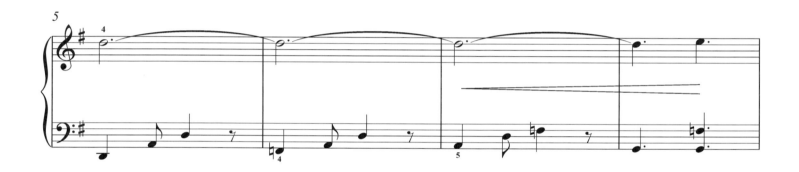

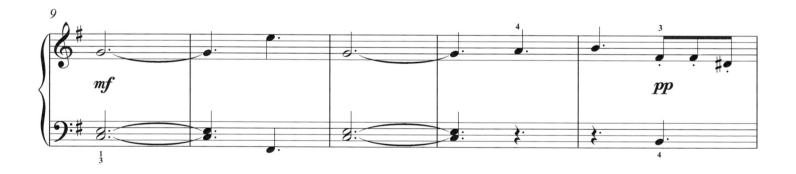

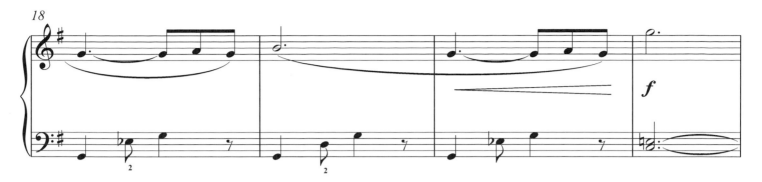

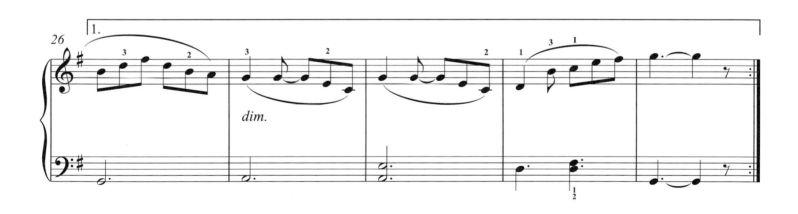

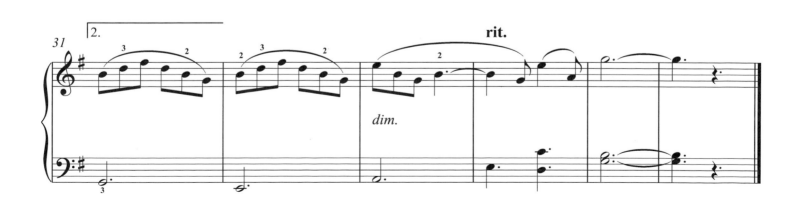

Symphony No. 9 'From the New World'

2nd movement

Antonín Dvořák
1841–1904

Pie Jesu

from Requiem

Gabriel Fauré
1845–1924

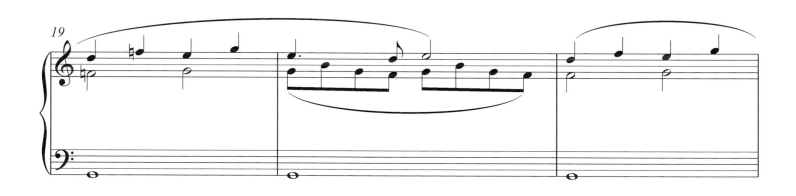

Panis Angelicus

César Franck
1822–1890

Poco lento

To Coda ⊕

D.C. al Coda

⊕ Coda

rit.

EDVARD
GRIEG

(1843–1907)

Edvard Grieg was the son of the English consul at Bergen, who was also a merchant. His mother was an accomplished pianist and possessed deep musical feeling.

When Grieg was seven years old, his mother started to teach him piano. She never praised him, but made him heed strictly to his work. He never liked to practise nor go to school and spent most of his time in dreams. This, of course, caused him no end of trouble with his mother and school teachers.

In 1858, violinist Ole Bull visited the Grieg home, and after reading Edvard's compositions urged him to go to the Leipzig Conservatory to become a musician. There, the following year, he studied harmony, piano, counterpoint and theory, composing throughout the period. In 1860, he broke down from overwork and went back to Norway, returning to Leipzig after a short absence.

In 1862, he again went to Norway, where he gave a successful concert of his own compositions. He continued to perform and compose extensively.

At the age of 27 he was invited by Liszt to Rome. Liszt gave tremendous praise to Grieg's compositions.

In 1874, Henrik Ibsen offered Grieg a contract to write the music to *Peer Gynt*. Its first performance was given in 1876 and was such a glorious success that it was played 36 times that year.

After this, Grieg made tours of London, Leipzig, Vienna, Paris and Copenhagen as a pianist, composer and conductor, and in some cases as all three. He was very well received wherever he appeared. His compositions include the famous *Peer Gynt* suite, his piano concerto, string quartet and many Norwegian songs.

Morning

from Peer Gynt

Edvard Grieg
1843–1907

Allegretto pastorale

Piano Concerto

1st movement

Edvard Grieg
1843–1907

Moderately fast

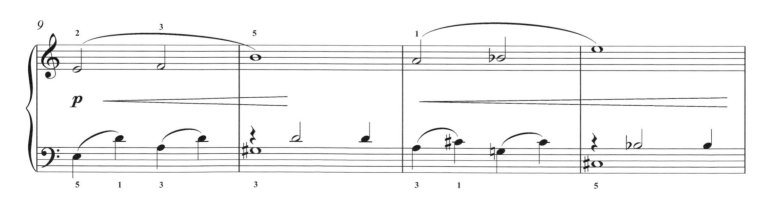

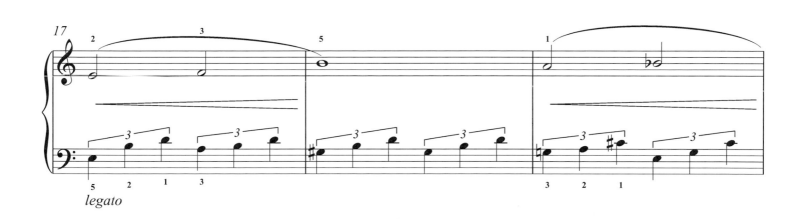

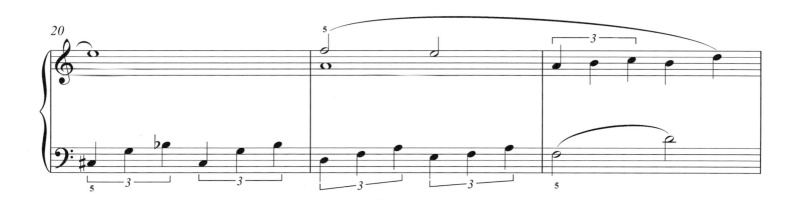

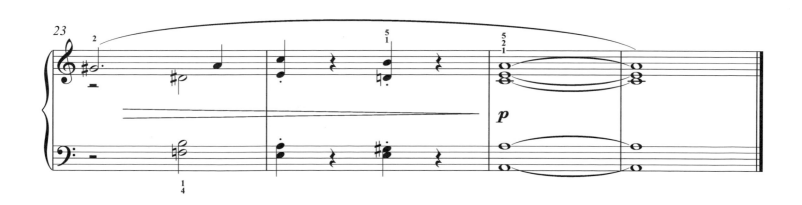

GEORGE FRIDERIC
HANDEL

(1685–1759)

Handel's childhood was marked by a strong passion for music, but his father, court physician to the Duke of Saxe-Meiningen, wishing him to become a lawyer, forbade him to have anything to do with music or musicians. However, sympathetic friends secretly procured an old spinet for him. This he hid in his attic and when everyone was asleep, he would pour his soul into it.

When he was seven years old, the Duke of Saxe-Wessenfels heard him play and urged his musical development. His father consented, and Handel began to study the oboe, spinet, harpsichord, organ and theory with Zachau, an organist.

In 1703, he went to Hamburg and became director of the orchestra the following year. During the ensuing two years of his stay, he composed three operas, the *St John Passion* and many smaller pieces. He visited Italy in 1706, where he was the guest of all the nobility. During a three year stay there he wrote about 150 solo cantatas, two oratorios and many operas. He then returned to Hanover and became conductor of the Orchestra of the Elector. In 1710, he went to London, where he was awaited impatiently by Queen Anne and her court. It was here that his opera *Rinaldo* was produced and met with tremendous success.

He continued writing operas, oratorios and all forms of sacred music. He lived most of the time in London, but occasionally made trips to Germany.

On April 13, 1742, his *Messiah* was introduced in Dublin. A year later it was produced in London and met with the greatest success ever accorded a musical composition. From that time on, Handel devoted himself largely to choral composition.

During the composition of *Jephtha*, a musical version of the biblical story, Handel was stricken with total blindness. Nevertheless, he kept on composing and played organ concerts, being led to and from the stage. He worked with unabated zeal until his sudden death, eight days after he conducted the final performance for that season, of his greatest work, *The Messiah*.

He is buried in the Poet's Corner of Westminster Abbey.

Hornpipe

from Water Music

George Frideric Handel
1685–1759

Brightly

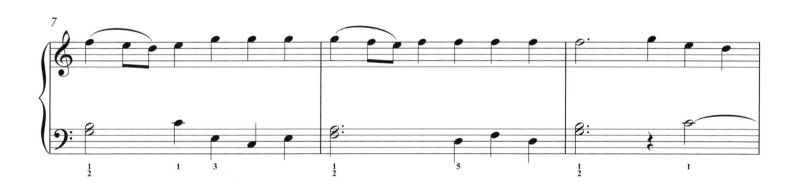

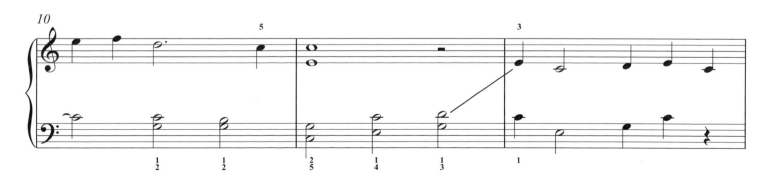

64

The Arrival of the Queen of Sheba

George Frideric Handel
1685–1759

Allegro

Lascia ch'io pianga

from Rinaldo

George Frideric Handel
1685–1759

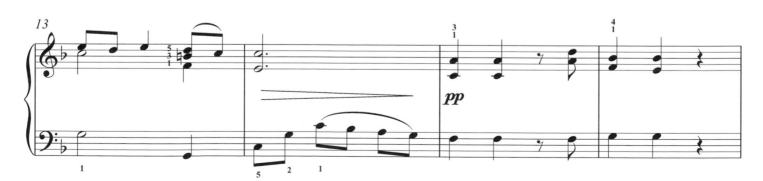

JOSEPH
HAYDN

(1732–1809)

Haydn's family history offers no clues to the huge fame he would achieve during his lifetime as one of the master composers of the Classical era. Born into a family of wheelwrights in the Austrian village of Rohrau on 31st March 1732, his roots lay in Hungary.

Haydn's father, himself an amateur musician, encouraged his son's talents. By the age of eight, Franz Joseph attended the choir school of St Stephen's Cathedral in Vienna, where he became one of the principial soloists, receiving tuition in harpsichord, violin and organ. At 18, Haydn was dismissed and supported himself through teaching, playing the organ and performing in orchestras and string quartets (he would later occasionally play with Mozart in a quartet).

In 1761 Haydn was appointed to a position in the household of the Esterházys, one of the wealthiest families in Austria. As music director, Haydn was given great support from Prince Nikolaus, a lover of music, who provided him with an excellent orchestra and artistic freedom. Works from these early years include 125 trios for viola, cello and baryton (a viol instrument) and various early comic operas. His output of courtly dances, numbering nearly 400, included the *12 Minuets*. His early string quartets, including the *Serenade*, also provided attractive court entertainment.

Following the death of Prince Nikolaus in 1970, Haydn was granted substantial leave, visiting London in 1791 and 1794, conducting weekly concerts and premiering new works. His last 12 symphonies were all composed for this trip, including the *'London' Symphony* (No. 104) and the *'Surprise' Symphony* (No. 94).

Back in Vienna, with a new prince in charge, Haydn resumed work in the household, writing his great masses, oratorios and quartets.

Haydn spent the last years of his life in retirement surrounded by the love of friends and other musicians. In May 1809, when Napoleon's armies invaded Vienna, Bonaparte himself ordered a guard to be placed outside the composer's home where he lay on his deathbed. He died on 31st May 1809 and is cherished as one of the great masters of composition.

Menuetto con Variazioni

from Sonata in D major

Joseph Haydn
1732–1809

Tempo di Menuetto

Symphony No. 104 'The London'

2nd movement

Joseph Haydn
1732–1809

Andante

Serenade

from String Quartet Op. 3, No. 5

Joseph Haydn
1732–1809

Jupiter

from The Planets

Gustav Holst
1874–1934

Andante maestoso

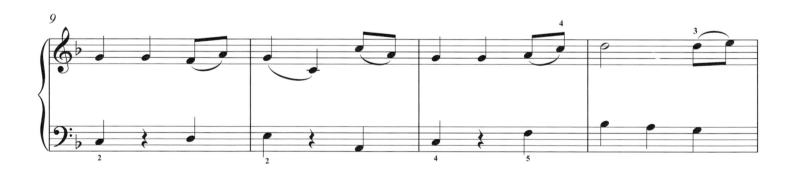

Liebestraum No. 3

Franz Liszt
1811–1886

Moderato

Méditation

from Thaïs

Jules Massenet
1842–1912

Andante ♩ = 66

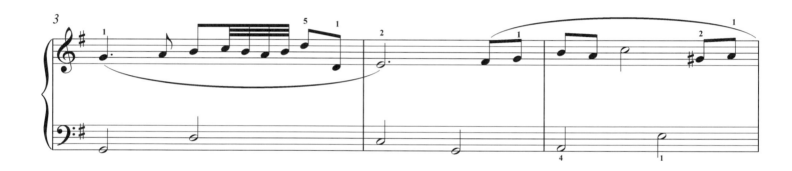

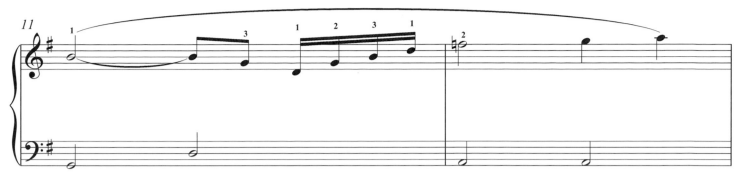

The Hebrides Overture

Fingal's Cave

Felix Mendelssohn
1809–1847

Moderato

WOLFGANG AMADEUS
MOZART

(1756–1791)

Wolfgang Amadeus Mozart was born in Salzburg, Austria on 27th January 1756. Though living a fairly short life, he is widely regarded as one of the most influential composers of all time.

Even as an infant, Mozart was learning music by ear and by the age of five was composing his own pieces. His father, Leopold, recognized these remarkable talents and took his children on a series of tours all over Europe. Mozart returned to Salzburg in 1766, having already written many compositions.

From 1769–77 Mozart, somewhat unbelievably, produced nearly 300 compositions, including over 20 symphonies. During this time he also toured to Italy, where he received a knighthood in Rome.

On 9th July 1772 Mozart become the Konzertmeister at the Salzburg Court. Mozart was frustrated at his attempts to leave Salzburg, though eventually managed to embark on a trip with his mother in 1777, visiting Mannheim and Paris. It was on this trip that he composed the variations on *Ah! Vous Dirai-je Maman*, the theme of which is better known as the nursery rhyme *Twinkle, Twinkle, Little Star*. Sadly, Mozart's mother Anna Maria died in Paris in 1778.

In 1782 he married Constanze Weber in St Stephen's Cathedral, having decided to settle permanently in Vienna. They went on to have six children, four of whom died in infancy. Despite this tragedy, Mozart's first years in Vienna were musically and financially very successful. Mozart was well known amongst his musical colleagues, including Joseph Haydn, who apparently told Leopold Mozart "before God, I tell you that your son is the greatest composer known to me in person or by reputation".

Despite his astonishing musical legacy of operas, symphonies, sonatas and many other pieces, Mozart fell into financial ruin, owing a lot of money, mostly to his Masonic brethren. In his final year, Mozart worked on three operas, the *Clarinet Concerto* and the *Requiem*, which remained unfinished at the time of his death in December 1791.

Mozart's remarkable influence stretched far and wide within his own lifetime and well into the centuries that followed his death.

Là ci darem la mano

from Don Giovanni

Wolfgang Amadeus Mozart
1756–1791

Moderato

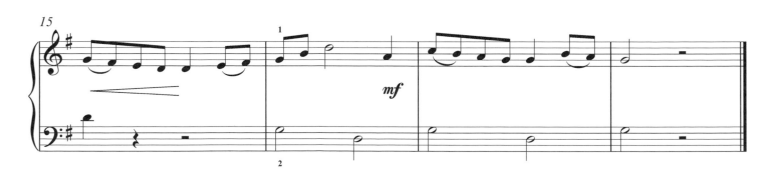

Sonata in A major

1st movement

Wolfgang Amadeus Mozart
1756–1791

Andante grazioso

Piano Concerto No. 21 in C major
'Elvira Madigan'
2nd movement

Wolfgang Amadeus Mozart
1756–1791

SERGEI
RACHMANINOFF

(1873–1943)

Sergei Rachmaninoff was born in a small village, Onega, in Novogorod. At a very early age he showed a decided inclination to music, especially the piano, and in 1882 was entered in the Petrograd Conservatory of Music, where he remained until 1885.

He then entered the Moscow Conservatory, where he studied the piano under Ziloti and composition under the famous Russian composers Arensky and Tanicff. His work here was so meritorious that he was awarded the Great Gold Medal for his excellence.

Having graduated from the conservatory in 189 he performed extensively and in 1899 was selected to serve in three capacities – pianist, composer and conductor to the London Philharmonic Society.

From then on, his life was marked by success in composition, conducting, piano recitals and teaching. From 1904 to 1906 he was conductor of the Imperial Opera in Moscow. After that, he moved to Dresden, where he devoted the greater part of his time to composition, occasionally engaging in concert tours.

His works include operas, songs, symphonies, piano concertos and piano pieces.

During a concert tour in 1942, Rachmaninoff fell ill and was diagnosed with advanced melanoma. He died on 28th March 1943, four days before his 70th birthday. A choir sang his All-Night Vigil at the funeral.

Piano Concerto No. 2

2nd movement

Sergei Rachmaninoff
1873–1943

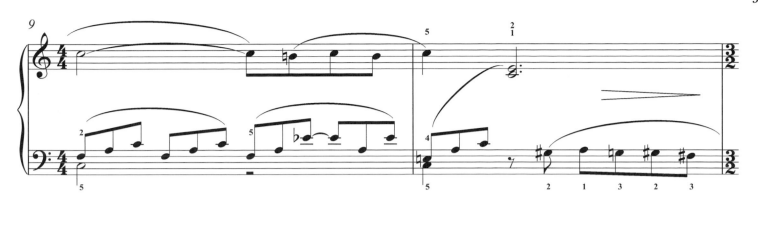

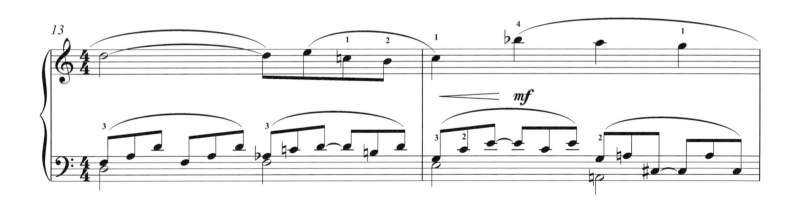

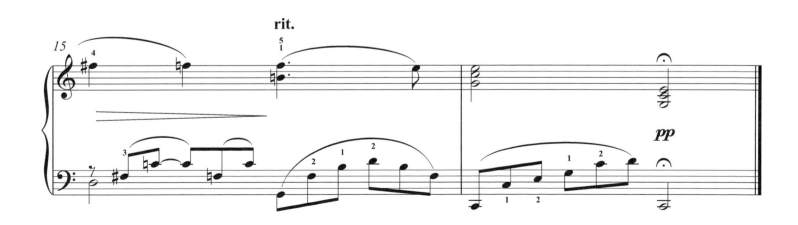

Piano Concerto No. 3

1st movement

Sergei Rachmaninoff
1873–1943

When I am laid in earth

from Dido and Aeneas

Henry Purcell
1659–1695

Larghetto

Domenico Scarlatti
1685–1757

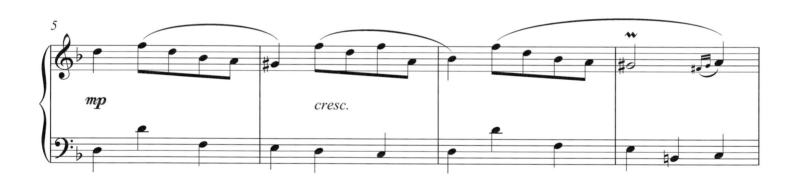

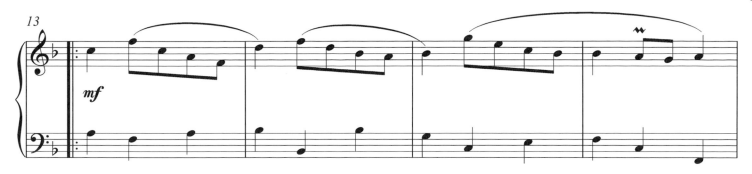

Entr'acte

from Rosamunde

Franz Schubert
1797–1828

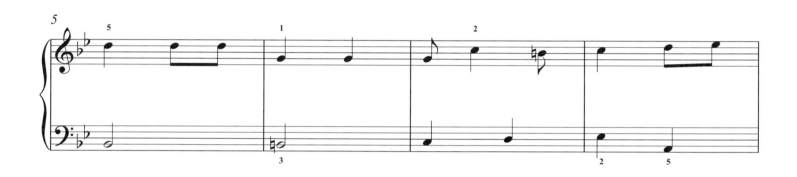

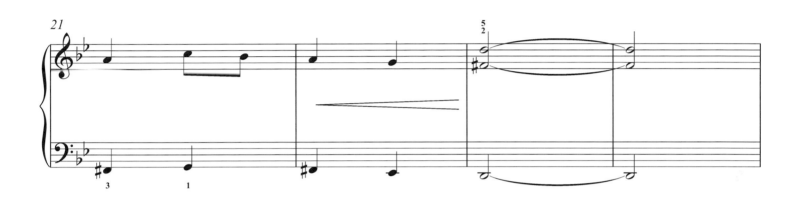

Ave Maria

Franz Schubert
1797–1828

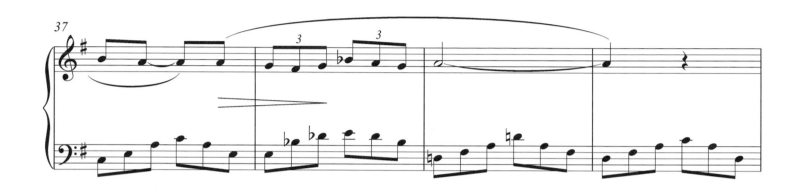

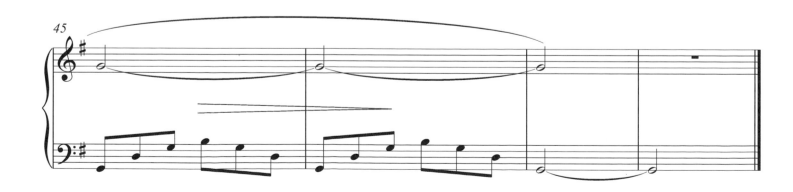

Death and the Maiden

from String Quartet No. 14 in D minor

Franz Schubert
1797–1828

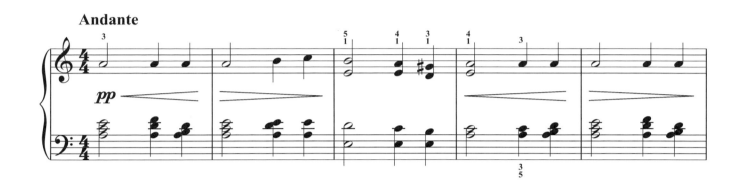

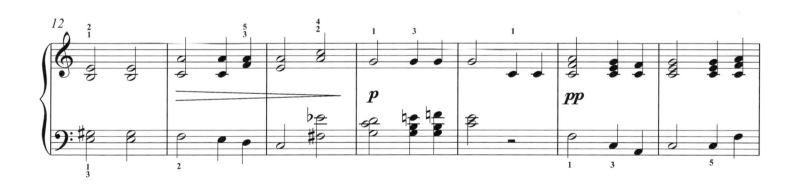

ROBERT
SCHUMANN

(1810–1856)

Robert Schumann's father was a publisher and owner of a book store in Zwickau. He was fairly well established. At the age of six, Robert was sent to a private school where he soon showed an inordinate fondness for music. His father allowed him to study music with Johann Gottfried Kuntsch, an organist.

At the age of seven, Robert was already composing little dances. From then, until he was 17, he developed along musical and literary lines. At this time, he made a concert appearance as a pianist. He won much applause, but his mother highly disapproved of a musical career, naming it a "breadless" calling. Not wishing to act contrary to her wishes he entered the University of Leipzig as a law student in 1828. Law and Schumann did not mix. While he was supposed to be studying torts or contracts he was instead practising on the piano.

When he was 20, his mother realised that it might be practical for him to be a musician. He devoted the rest of his life to music, as pianist, composer and musical editor.

While studying with Wieck he met Clara, his daughter, who later became the passion of his life. A short time later, Schumann lamed one of his fingers through faulty practising and was obliged to give up his piano playing. After this, he kept on composing and also became editor of a very progressive musical paper.

He made the acquaintance of Chopin, Mendelssohn, Wagner and Liszt, the latter becoming a great factor in the popularisation of Schumann's compositions by playing them frequently at his concerts.

He composed a great many songs, sonatas, symphonies, fantasies, concertos and other works.

His work was constantly being interrupted by nervous disorders, said to have been inherited from his father. In 1854 he broke down and was lodged in an asylum, where he remained until he died.

Soldier's March

from Album For The Young

Robert Schumann
1810–1856

Träumerei

from Album For The Young

Robert Schumann
1810–1856

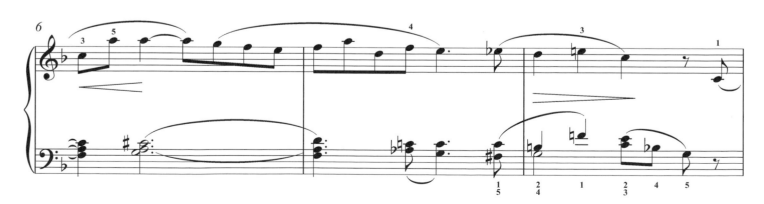

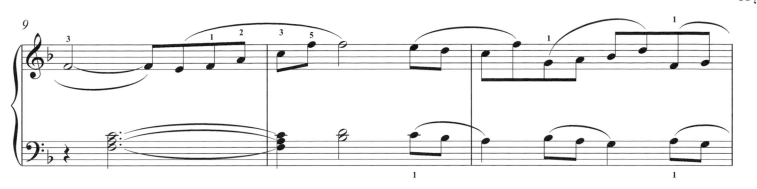

rit.   a tempo

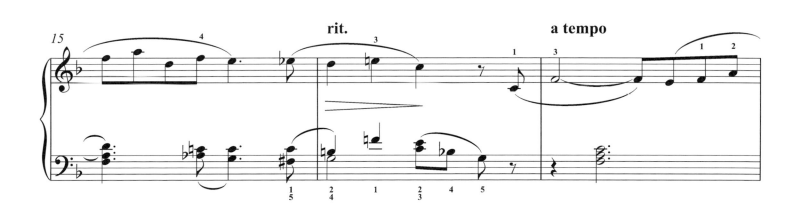

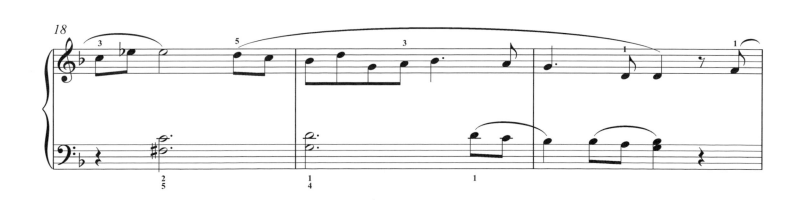

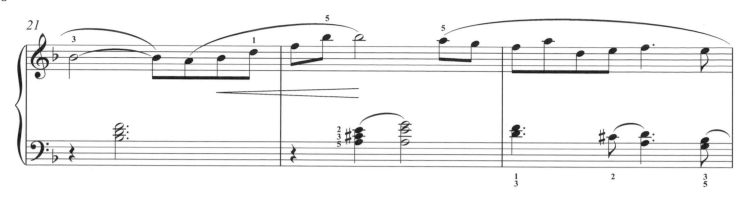

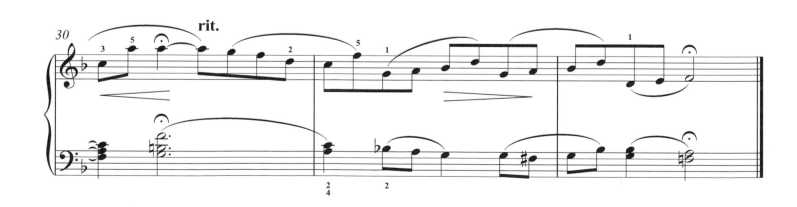

Tales from the Vienna Woods

Johann Strauss
1825–1899

Moderato

Emperor Waltz

Johann Strauss
1825–1899

PYOTR ILYICH
TCHAIKOVSKY

(1840–1903)

Pyotr Ilyich Tchaikovsky was the son of a civil engineer employed by the Russian government. He was interested in music from the age of four years old, but was not permitted to develop this interest until he was ten. At that time, he was placed in a school in St Petersburg to be prepared for the study of law and was given piano lessons privately. The death of his mother in 1854 was a great shock to him and is said to have been the cause of the melancholy character of his compositions.

Upon graduation from Law School in 1859, he became an official of the Department of Justice, but, not being particularly interested in his work, he devoted his spare time to music. Two years later he started serious study of composition in the St Petersburg Conservatory and in 1864 was appointed Professor of Theory and Composition at the Moscow Conservatory.

In 1877, he formed a friendship with a wealthy widow, Madame Nadeshda von Meck, who, being interested in his compositions, granted him an annual income of 6,000 rubles so that he could devote all his time to composition. The remarkable circumstance of this incident is that he never met his benefactor personally but conducted correspondence with her.

For the next 10 years, he devoted himself almost exclusively to composition, producing during this time three symphonies, several operas, a violin concerto, the 1812 Overture, the Nutcracker Suite and many other smaller pieces.

He was friendly with Brahms and Grieg. In 1891, he directed the New York Philharmonic in a concert of his own compositions with great success.

He died of cholera ten days after the first performance of *Symphony No. 6.*

Piano Concerto No. 1 in B♭ major

1st movement

Pyotr Ilyich Tchaikovsky
1840–1893

Allegro non troppo

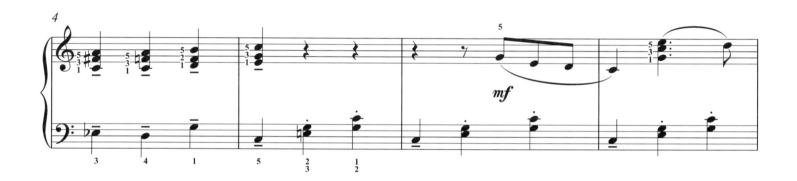

Waltz of the Flowers

from The Nutcracker Suite

Pyotr Ilyich Tchaikovsky
1840–1893

Tempo di valse moderato

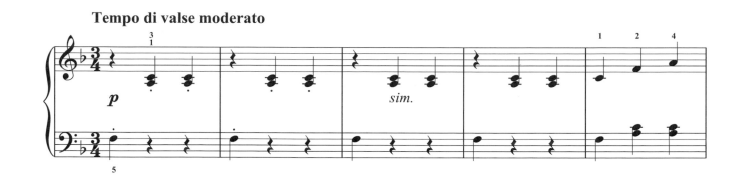

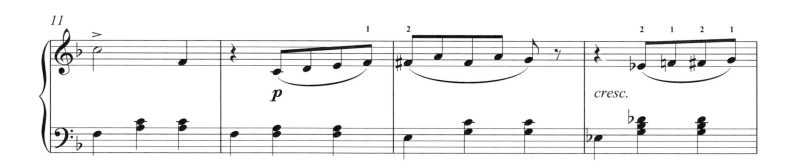

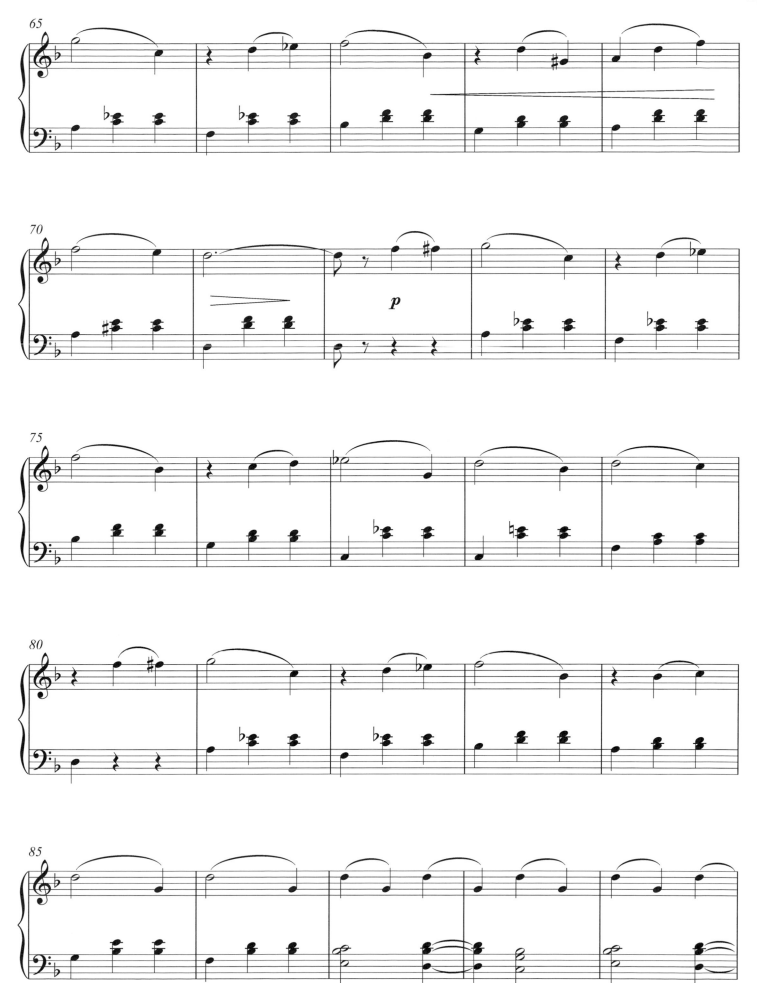

Pathétique Symphony

1st Movement

Pyotr Ilyich Tchaikovsky
1840–1893

Danse Galante

Georg Philipp Telemann
1681–1767

Autumn

from The Four Seasons

Antonio Vivaldi
1678–1741

Allegro

La donna è mobile

from Rigoletto

Giuseppe Verdi
1813–1901

Chorus of the Hebrew Slaves

from Nabucco

Giuseppe Verdi
1813–1901

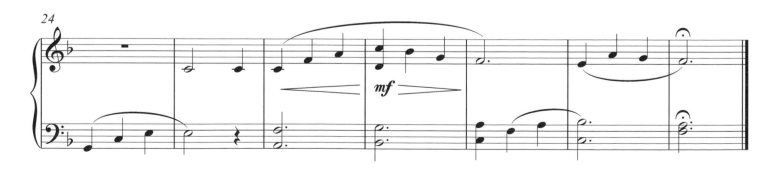